Create Your Community

A Young Adult's Guide to Successful Networking

Fifth Anniversary Edition

Scott Rubenstein

For Mom, Dad, and Zachary

For all the communities I've been blessed to be a part of, including my extended family, the Arizona Jewish Theatre Company, NFTY, URJ Kutz Camp, and the University of Pennsylvania

For everyone in my network who has shown me kindness and generosity with their time, knowledge, and connections as I navigate my career

In loving memory of my grandparents: Zelda Perlman, Julius and Trudi Rubenstein, and Warren Perlman

Edited by Cameron Kiszla

Edited by Robin Rubenstein and Dan Rubenstein

Special Thanks to Brianna Raposo

Table of Contents

Introduction to the Fifth Anniversary Edition

It's been five years since *Create Your Community* was released, and in many ways, it feels as though the world has been through enough to fill 50 years. We emerged from a global pandemic that killed millions. The January 6, 2021 insurrection, Russia's invasion of Ukraine in 2022, Hamas's October 7, 2023 attack on Israel and the ongoing war, the 2024 U.S. presidential election, and other events make young adults like me feel discombobulated and helpless. My community of supportive collaborators and allies is what has helped me feel grounded in turbulent times and has provided a solid base to anchor me when I have felt like things have been out of my control. I have certainly learned a lot from my community since this book was published, and with their help I have made significant positive changes to my life's trajectory.

Shortly after this book was published in 2020, I decided to pivot away from pursuing a career in the entertainment industry, on which I had been doggedly focused throughout college. I had been furloughed from my job due to the pandemic, so I had a daunting amount of free time to figure out my next steps. It was time to lean on my network. I had an inkling that crisis communication sounded interesting, so I reached out to my college career center to see if there were alumni that would be willing to talk to me about the industry. I also reached out to family members, my friends' parents, friends of my friends' parents, and a myriad of other second and third-degree connections to learn all I could about the landscape of a completely new industry. I conducted almost 75 informational interviews. After many months, I landed a new job at a strategic communication firm in New York City, and I relocated there from Los Angeles in 2021.

Meanwhile, I tried some different networking experiments during this time. I reached out to a different person in my network every single day in 2021, with no repeats. I found it rewarding to reconnect with many friends during a time of isolation, but as someone who loves connecting, it was not as effortless as I expected. There were many days where I was too busy, or did not feel like I had someone in mind that I wanted to reach out to. I developed a newfound appreciation for those for whom networking is unnatural, while feeling reinvigorated to establish and maintain as many meaningful connections as I can. Then, for a little over two years, I stopped using all social media except for LinkedIn. I did not open Facebook, Instagram, Twitter/X or Snapchat. While not my original intention, it became a fun challenge to continue keeping in touch with friends intentionally and proactively. During this time, I also made many new friends in New York City. Not using social media allowed me to form real connections and to be thoughtful about following up and following through.

My experiences with networking since this book was first released in 2020 have only strengthened my passion for it and my belief in its essentiality. At the time, we were all experiencing an intense isolation from each other which took a toll on our collective mental health. Even though we made efforts to connect virtually throughout this difficult time, video conference calls could not replace the sense of community we get from being together in person. Though we have moved on from that period, somehow the isolation persists.

In 2023, U.S. Surgeon General Dr. Vivek Murthy issued an advisory on the "loneliness epidemic," expressing concern about the way social media negatively affects the mental health of young people. It seems we have never been more connected, and yet we have never felt lonelier. This issue appears to be particularly acute among young men, who are less likely than women to have close friends, stable employment or a college degree. Several prominent voices like Dr. Richard Reeves and Scott Galloway have written and spoken thoughtfully about the state of young men today. As a young man myself, I know that a big portion of the happiness and satisfaction I have with life comes from meaningful relationships with others. Having a community is important not just for professional endeavors, which is a prominent focus of this book, but for personal happiness.

Another major development since this book's original publication is the rapidly growing influence of artificial intelligence (AI) in everyday life. The presence of AI in audio, visual, and written communication has proliferated in ways that both help us become more efficient in our daily tasks but can confuse our ability to decipher reality from misinformation. Alarmingly, AI is also beginning to stand in for human relationships. In 2024, a teen committed suicide after allegedly being encouraged to do so by an AI chatbot with which he had developed an intimate relationship. While this is an extreme example, it nevertheless reminds us that as powerful as AI is or will be, it will never be human, and therefore it can never replace the human experience. Networking runs on the language learning model of human-to-human interactions, using communication to make an impact on others and to form relational bonds between people. The connections between humans are made and maintained by humans. Though AI can be an aid, *you* must create your community.

One of my networking heroes is the late David Rockefeller, former chairman of Chase Manhattan Bank. With the help of staff, over his lifetime he meticulously maintained a giant Rolodex of about 200,000 people. He also used this pre-digital contact list to keep notes of the dates and details of his interactions. If he was to see someone again, he'd review their Rolodex card(s) as a reminder and then bring up this information and appear as though he had an excellent memory while putting the person at ease. I can imagine it would be incredibly touching if I had the opportunity to meet him, tell him about this book, and he asked about it the next time I saw him, years later. This was an incredible way to make an impact on others and maintain relationships. I am inspired by this high-caliber networking and try my best to emulate it. If I've learned anything in the last five years, it is that nothing brings a sense of belonging, comfort and happiness like having a community. I intend to create the largest community I can, and I hope you will too.

Scott Rubenstein, 2025

Foreword from the Author

This book is being published amidst the 2019-2020 coronavirus (COVID-19) global pandemic. The threat of the coronavirus has upended our society in ways that severely affect how we interact with each other. Restaurants and coffee shops are closed or are operating at limited capacity. Most office-based companies have employees working from home. The term "social distancing" is now a part of our daily vernacular.

We don't know what the future holds or what kind of lasting impact the pandemic will have. One thing that will never change is our need to have strong communities around us. We are lucky that we have the technology to make meaningful connections without physical proximity. The strategies discussed in this book are still necessary and useful for effective networking. If you are reading this book with these circumstances in mind, note ways to use the information in compliance with physical distancing guidelines. Hopefully, the following pages will be just as helpful.

Regards,
Scott Rubenstein

Introduction—What is Networking?

As young adults, whether students or new to the workforce, we often hear the same cynical tidbit from our elders: it's not what you know, it's who you know.

What an utterly aggravating thing to hear. We spend virtually our entire lives to date in school learning math, science, English, foreign languages, history, and the like in order to make it in this world as adults. When we cry out, "When am I ever going to use linear algebra in real life?" we are told that it is foundational, and that education is the key to success. In my freshman English classroom in high school, my teacher had a poster on the wall labeled "justification for a higher education" that showed a large mansion overlooking a beautiful lake, a helicopter, a boat, and a garage filled with five expensive cars. I saw that image every day. When I was struggling to recall the tiniest details of *The Iliad* during the test, it would inspire me to keep pushing through.

This message is reinforced all through school, but then at the end, we're told that education actually isn't as important; instead, it's mainly that we know the right people who can help us. How demoralizing!

Obviously, that's not entirely true. Education *is* important. One *does* need knowledge in order to succeed. Once you get a job, you have to be able to keep it, and so of course knowledge and skills are vital to an effective performance. However, the part about who you know is also very important. In a globalized world where more people are going to college than ever before, competition in the job market is fierce. Often, to get a leg up, you have to know the right people. In some cases, it is essential.

That can be tough to hear because that means the world is not a meritocracy. Yes, the best and most qualified people very often win in the end, but those people most likely did not get there alone. They knew the right people along the way. Sometimes, because of a connection, the most qualified person loses out to someone who may not have deserved it. While that can be frustrating, that's often how the game is played. Why not play it too?

I know the above all sounds cynical, but playing the game—the game of networking, that is—is actually very fun. Connecting with other people can be very rewarding, and early in your career, it is one of the best ways to *learn*. Ah, so it is what you know after all! It makes sense, doesn't it? Yeah, y=mx+b probably won't help you in the real world, but there's knowledge out there that *will* help you that you cannot learn in school. Your network is the place to get such information.

So, what is networking? I believe it's **the work of creating and building a community of supportive collaborators and allies with common interests who desire to share in each other's success.** Even without realizing it, you do it every day and have done it since before you can remember. Everyone you know, from your boss at work, your professors at school, to even your immediate family are in your network.

Who am I?

Before we go any further, I'd like to share a little about me and why I'm writing this book. I was born in Phoenix, Arizona, and was raised like most other middle-class kids. I went to public school, participated in extracurricular activities, and was involved in my religious community. Fortunately, I have two parents who were able to provide everything I needed growing up. Our family was close with extended relatives and we had friends in various organizations in our community.

In high school, I participated in a Jewish sleepaway camp in New York, the now-defunct URJ Kutz Camp, where I met other Jewish teens from all over the country. I was also involved in the Reform Jewish teen movement NFTY, serving on its North American board my senior year of high school. When it came time to apply to colleges, I had a lot of knowledge about what it is like to attend a wide array of schools because I knew people at schools all over the country. I chose to attend the University of Pennsylvania in Philadelphia, a school thousands of miles away from my home in Arizona, in part because I knew people who had gone there before me. Through those connections, I was able to learn enough about Penn to know that it was the right school for me.

Since my sophomore year of high school, I knew I wanted to work in the entertainment industry, specifically in television, but I didn't know much about what it takes to break into the business. In addition, my college did not have a strong connection to the entertainment industry like it did other industries. Investment banks and consulting firms would send representatives to campus to recruit in person. Entertainment companies did not visit campus and barely did any recruiting at all. I had to figure out how it all works and where to start. In the near term, I wanted an entertainment internship in either Los Angeles or New York, but I knew they were highly competitive. The people who got those positions usually had a close and powerful connection that helped them, something I lacked.

Based on advice from Penn's career services advising, I combed through our online alumni network and started cold emailing people working in the industry. I asked them for 20 minutes of their time to hop on the phone and tell me about their experiences. From there, I began building a network of people from whom I have learned a ton about the industry. As time passed, I quickly discovered that many people in my life knew people who worked in the industry. My family and friends eagerly offered to connect me with *their* friends and family to learn more.

At school, I became involved in the Wharton Undergraduate Media and Entertainment Club as the professional development chair, and then the vice president. I found myself advising other students on how to use their network to meet the right people and learn more about the industry. I've come to understand just how vital all of this is for success in the early stages of a career.

So why am I writing this book? Yes, networking books exist, but this one is specifically geared toward learning to use networking when in school or early in your career. When you have little or no work experience, it is your network that helps you get your foot in the door. This book is about my philosophy of networking and what I have learned about it along the way. I am in my early career too. In fact, as of this writing, I'm still at my first job in the entertainment industry. Who better to discuss networking with when you're first starting out than someone who is also still starting out?

This book will explore networking as a concept and hopefully destigmatize it. It will describe and explain how to find the people you want to know, how to reach out and make a connection, and how to keep that connection for years to come. It will identify some of the harsh realities about networking that make it an admittedly inequitable system and find ways of overcoming built-in disadvantages in the networking game. This book, in and of itself, is a great example of networking. Many of the skills, tips, and tricks provided reflect what I have learned from thoughtful and generous people whom I have had the pleasure of getting to know. Hopefully, this book will give you the tools you need to connect with people, advance your career, and help advance the career of others. Don't forget, it always works both ways!

Thank you for joining me on this journey, and happy networking!

Why is Networking Important?

We are naturally social creatures, so it only makes sense that we work better together. We like knowing people and having people know us. We are more willing to do work with people that we trust, and the first step to trust is establishing a connection.

Much of the work done in the workforce is relationship driven. Any kind of service provider who makes a living from their skills has established relationships with their clients who trust them. In many cases, people rely on "word of mouth" to keep their business going. That's all networking! People such as real estate agents, handymen, and party planners rely on clients to tell their networks about their good experiences with the service provider. Investors taking on new projects, such as in real estate or a start-up, raise capital from other investors they know. Journalists, especially those who cover politics, do their work by developing good, trusting relationships with their sources. If an anonymous source gives information to a journalist, they must have complete trust that their identity will be protected. Without a network of relationships, there would be very little access to what is happening behind the scenes in Washington, D.C. or at the state capitol.

In short, networking is what makes the world go round. When you're established in any field, using your network can make the difference in achieving your professional objectives, whether it be a small project or starting a new division in your company. Many books explain how and why this is important for well-established professionals. What about those just starting out?

Why is Networking Important for Young People?

In a world where people are more willing and more likely to do business with people they know and trust, an unknown entity such as a young person fresh out of school is a much bigger hiring risk. There is little or no track record with which to judge how an inexperienced person will perform on the job. If there are multiple candidates with similar backgrounds, how do employers decide who to hire?

Imagine you work for an ad agency and you're looking to hire a new young employee for an entry-level position. You have a large stack of resumes in front of you, and most of them have the same universities, same GPAs, same majors, and no standout extracurriculars. You can't interview all of them; you just want to interview the ones who you think are the best applicants. How can you even choose?

Now imagine your biggest client calls and says that they know an applicant who is applying for that job. The client says that this one applicant was an altar boy at his church and is super smart, very creative, and was well-liked in the church community. "You should interview him," the client says. How would you react? Well, first of all, this is your biggest client, so you don't want to upset him. Is it a bit of favor to interview this kid? Maybe, but he is an applicant after all, and while he may not stand out from the pack on paper, his knowing the client differentiates himself enough that it warrants an interview. Just like that, someone's resume gets pulled from the stack because of who they know.

It's important to note that the connection does not guarantee the ad agency will necessarily hire the applicant. He still has to interview and sell himself, as he should. I do not mean to suggest you can coast on by as long as you know the right people. Absolutely not. This applicant needs to have the skills and the talent to seal the deal and secure the job. However, without that connection, he might not have interviewed at all.

Networking is important in your early career because we live in a hypercompetitive, globalized world where no matter how hard you try, it's very difficult to stand out on a resume or application. Knowing the right people may give just the right amount of boost you need to take the baton and run across the finish line. It's the network that separates you from the pack.

After all, you worked hard in school and in extracurriculars to get where you want to go. Wouldn't you want to do everything you can to make sure all your hard work pays off? The problem is that networking has developed a bad reputation among young people, which is understandable. As we will discuss, networking isn't always used for good. However, in my opinion, people who feel negatively about networking aren't looking at it the right way.

Networking's Bad Reputation and Why It's Undeserved

In college, it became clear to me the majority of people who actually enjoyed the process of networking were business students. They had LinkedIn accounts before freshman year, they eagerly attended "networking events" (more on these later), and they were not shy about trying to use connections to help achieve their professional goals. Non-business students also recognized the value of networking but more often seemed to find it a chore, a burden, and a skill they declared themselves "not good at."

Some people were anti-networking. They associated it with elitism and corporate greed and actually refused to engage in it. I can understand networking having a slimy reputation if one is doing it the wrong way. Yes, there is a right and wrong way to network. I'm sure many people are networking poorly by being haphazard, uncaring, and selfishly pursuing their own interests. These networkers often make big asks of strangers without taking the time to get to know them, and they show little willingness to help anyone else if they fear competition. If you don't network the right way, you will not be effective, and you will not create a community of allies.

No Quid Pro Quo!

Networking should not be transactional. The "I'll do this for you if you do that for me" mentality is not conducive to building a strong network. The goal should be to have a genuine, human relationship with the people in your network. If your networking is built on quid pro quos and striking deals, then people won't really care about helping you and you won't care about helping them. A lot of people see networking this way, and it's understandable that they wouldn't like it if that's all they think it is.

We all know that guy who got his nephew a job because someone owed him a favor. That's not great networking; that is a transaction built on obligation and guilt. It's the idea that if someone does something for me, then I need to repay the favor somehow in the future, and I'll feel guilty if I don't. Quid pro quos create liabilities and debts. You shouldn't ever be in "networking debt," owing favors to people who have helped you. People who expect such a repayment are not true allies and are not worth having in your network anyway.

A good networker gives selflessly. I help people when I can because I want to, not because I expect anything in return. Naturally, people want to help others who would help them, so it's not one-sided either. There should be giving and receiving on both sides of the equation, but it's usually not a perfect tit-for-tat and shouldn't be.

Sometimes, people will say, "I owe you one." That is relatively harmless because it's natural to feel like you should repay someone who has been kind and helpful. If anything, "owing one" should be done from a place of gratitude, not guilt. Quid pro quos are not a healthy foundation for a meaningful relationship.

There's No Shame...Really

Some people think networking carries a shameful stigma. If you use networking to get a job, that must mean you didn't actually deserve it. You didn't earn it based on your own merit; you called in a favor. This isn't true! It's a competitive world and sometimes you need a connection to help you achieve your goals even though you deserve to achieve them anyway!

I think people confuse networking with nepotism, the practice of those in power favoring close friends and relatives, even if they aren't the most qualified for the opportunities they're obtaining. This is a type of networking, but the *vast* majority of networking is not nepotism! Doing the work to build a community of people who care about you and want to help you should not carry any shame with it. If one of those people in your network helps you get a job or achieve another goal, you should be proud, not ashamed.

Nepotism is undeniably unfair to those who don't benefit from it, and it is one of the reasons networking has a bad reputation. However, there's so much more to networking than nepotism. I also understand that sometimes networking can highlight inequities in society. Some of the harsh realities of networking will be confronted in a later chapter.

Networking for Social Change

Don't forget that networking is an important part of social justice! Developing and building social movements takes networking to help amass enough power to be effective. Think of all the biggest social justice movements of the last several decades. People got involved in these causes either because they heard about them directly in their social circles or they learned through media coverage. If the media is covering a social movement, they've become popular enough to be noticeable.

Today, social media plays a huge role in this type of organizing. Between three and six million people showed up in Washington, D.C. for the Women's March on January 21, 2017. How did so many people know that the march was happening? How did they know where and when to go? Word spread through networks of like-minded people on social media. In response to the tragic 2020 murder of George Floyd at the hands of Minneapolis police officers, protests and even rioting broke out all over the country. How were people able to organize effectively in each city from coast to coast? People spread the word through their social networks.

This is even more impressive when you consider how these movements organized before the advent of social media. How did Martin Luther King Jr. manage to get hundreds of thousands of people to march with him in Washington, D.C. back in 1963? Social media didn't exist, communication was tough, and information was scarce. The power of the message was strong enough that it spread through social networks and successfully amassed a movement.

Importantly, these are examples of one-off events. On a more continuous basis, movements are built, supported, and sustained using networking and community organizing. While we often think of networking in terms of professional development, it's important to remember it's used for social justice as well.

Networking at its Best

Revisiting the definition of networking that I offered at the beginning, it is **the work of creating and building a community of supportive collaborators and allies with common interests who desire to share in each other's success**. Let's break that down a bit.

- **Work**—Building and maintaining a dynamic network does not just happen on its own. It takes time, effort, and thought to cultivate. Later in this book, work will be explained in detail.

- **Creating and building a community**—In a community, no one member is more important than another. Although one's position may be more important, every member in a community has value and brings something worthwhile to the table. Your network is not all about you. You are creating a community around you, and you are part of the communities of everyone else in your network.

- **Supportive collaborators**—You create a network to work together. Whether it's writing a screenplay, preparing for a group presentation, or seeking advice from a respected acquaintance, a network supports each other and collaborates whenever possible.

- **Allies**—I have observed that some people feel that in order to achieve success, they must be willing to make a few enemies on their way to the top. I reject this. Whenever possible, you should strive to *avoid* making enemies. You never know when you will want to work with someone down the road. Of course, you should always stand up for your values and principles. Occasionally, making an enemy is unavoidable, but that will seldom occur. Having an ally is always better than having an enemy.

- **Common Interests**—The most valuable members of a network will be people with whom you have common interests, such as those in your professional field. These are the people from whom to learn the most and obtain the best opportunities. This may seem obvious, but it is definitely important to be able to distinguish to whom you want to devote most of your time and effort getting to know. I certainly have many people in my network who don't share many common interests with me, but that's okay because that could change down the road. You never know who you will cross paths with again.

• **Desire to share in each other's success—** This is vitally important to a successful network, because a strong network will never form without it. Networking *cannot* be self-serving. A truly successful network means that you are as invested in everyone else's success as much as you hope they are invested in yours. It is always a two-way street.

At the Jewish camp I attended in New York, the director instilled in the campers and staff a set of values that I have taken to heart and try to live by every day. I use these values to inform my networking. I am grateful to camp for teaching me so much about how to live my life with meaning, including the way I conduct my networking.

One of these principles is **the value of every human being**. Every person is the most important person in the world to someone, and they deserve to be treated as such. When you think of every person you meet as the most important person in the world, you will automatically become interested in knowing what they know. You'll treat them with the utmost respect and dignity, and they will do the same for you. In turn, they will become invested in your success as well.

Another one of these values is **compassion**. We don't know everything that is going on in someone else's life. Everyone goes through rough times and that's okay. It is important to give people space when they need it. Along with compassion, it is important to always **assume goodwill**. If you reach out to someone new and they don't reply, assume that they want to but are too busy. It may just be a bad time. Don't assume they don't like you or don't want to talk to you. It takes a lot less effort to be kind than unkind. Believe that everyone is **being their best, and you should do the same and accept the rest.** It is important to recognize that your personal best may not be to the same standard as someone else's and that's okay. "Best" is different for everyone.

Internalizing these values is easier said than done, but I believe it starts with emotional intelligence, or EQ, which I'd argue is more important than IQ when it comes to navigating the world and being successful. The ability to correctly identify the emotions of both yourself and others is important for having empathy and being a helpful ally.

These values which I learned at camp are the building blocks of successful networking. They serve as the foundation for a community of supportive collaborators and allies. Building a community rooted in these values is what networking looks like at its best: a compassionate, emotionally intelligent community that shares in the joy of everyone's success.

We All Network Without Realizing It

As noted, throughout college, many of my friends would say they "hate" networking, they're really bad at it, or it's too much work. Networking became characterized in a way that made it seem like a dirty deed, something only the greediest people would do to get what they want. Actually, networking is something everyone does every single day, often without realizing it!

A formal business deal is a very different type of interaction than two friends hanging out, but in both scenarios, networking is taking place. Human relationships are the building blocks of a network. Wouldn't it stand to reason that all the people you know are in your network already? And by interacting with them, wouldn't you be networking?

Think about what the word community means. You don't have to look up an exact definition to know it's a grouping of people who have some sort of commonality, whether it be proximity, religion, or another interest or value. If you have a family, if you go to or have gone to a school, if you are a part of an extracurricular activity or religious organization, or if you live in a neighborhood, you are part of a community.

Think about our working definition of networking. The first part of it alludes to the "work of creating and building community." As a child, communities get created and built for you. If you're born into a family with siblings, some parental figures, and extended relatives, you're a part of a community.

My mother's side of the family certainly lives this concept of community. My maternal grandmother was one of five siblings and all the descendants of all those five siblings make a huge effort to be a part of each other's lives. We are spread out all over the country, but whenever there is a wedding or a B'nai Mitzvah, we all show up. My grandmother and her siblings were born and raised in Mobile, Alabama, so Southern hospitality is a big part of our family culture. At all major family events, we stay at the same hotel and rent out a suite we call the "hospitality room." Everyone brings homemade baked goods to share and throughout the weekend, the hospitality room is the community center. With any free time, the family is in the hospitality room, noshing away and catching up on each other's lives. The socializing goes late into the night. All ages, from 8 to 80, hang out there. We have other family traditions as well, such as Thanksgivings at my great aunt and uncle's house in Alabama and our Hanukkah name-draw, when we're all assigned another family member to give a gift to during the holidays. All spouses who marry into the family are welcomed with open arms and are treated as family immediately. While many people don't even know who their second cousins are, I grew up with them as close family members because our grandparents instilled the importance of family in us from a young age. Now, I fully recognize that my family's hospitality room arrangement is a very special situation, and not many families operate like this. However, I know many people from big families and small families alike who share a strong sense of community in their own special ways.

Beyond your family, what other early-life networks did you encounter? Most likely, you went to school with other kids your age. Think about your elementary school classes. Day in and day out, you spent time with the same group of about 25-30 kids and a teacher. Those classrooms were certainly communities! Maybe you can't now remember who was in each class, but at the time, you shared many common experiences every single day.

Obviously, as elementary school students, we weren't helping each other advance career objectives, but we were experiencing something interesting together and creating a shared memory. I guarantee that if I talked to any of my fourth-grade classmates today, we would reminisce about that day we made solar ovens out of pizza boxes and tin foil to learn about convection. It's a commonality that ties us together. Having memorable shared experiences like our solar ovens naturally forms stronger bonds among people. No matter how often I talk to my classmates, we have that shared history, and so we are in each other's networks.

In addition to these two initial ones, you have done the work of building communities of *your* choice without realizing it. If you had a group of close friends at school, that's a community as well. If you were a part of an extracurricular activity or club, you self-selected into a community of people with a shared interest.

I've always been fascinated by group chats, whether via text, Facebook, or Snapchat. These chats are a way to keep a group of friends or family together, often from a long distance. It can be a very important way to maintain relationships. I have a group chat with my immediate family, which is helpful because both my brother and I have moved out of the house. It allows us to communicate easily. I have a group chat with five of my closest friends from camp, and often it is what gets me through the day. When I want opinions on something, usually the first place I turn to is my camp group chat. Your group chats are communities!

When I was a kid, I was involved in musical theatre. Every summer between the ages of 7 and 15, I attended a four-week-long theatre day camp. We spent all day rehearsing for a show and learning different theatre concepts. Theatre kids can't help but bond with castmates, and the 30 or so of us involved with the camp became a community. I distinctly remember everyone crying at the end of the camp session because we wouldn't be seeing each other daily anymore. However, the bond remains, and some of my longest lasting friendships are from theatre camp. Also, the director was one of the most influential adults in my childhood, and I still look up to her.

There's a similar type of camaraderie in sports. I played sports as a very young child, but those who continued playing on teams in middle school and high school probably relate to my theatre community experience. Teammates spend hours practicing with the same people, playing their hearts out against their rivals, and sometimes even traveling together for games and tournaments. There's no work involved in building this community. It happens as a natural byproduct of a common interest.

Religion also places a high level of import on building community, and is often very explicit about it. In life's most important milestones, whether it be birth, marriage, or death, religion is there for you. When a community member passes away, for example, a church may organize its members to make dinners for the family in their time of grief. In traditional Jewish communities, some religious services require ten participants be present to proceed. Some prayers literally cannot be said without a community present!

As mentioned, in high school I was very involved with my Jewish youth organization on the North American level and attended the organization's camp in New York. I started at my temple youth group and at the regional level, building a community with other Jewish teens in Arizona, New Mexico, Las Vegas, Nevada and El Paso, Texas. We had regional weekend events four times a year and the message was clear: this organization, NFTY-Southwest, is about building community. We would often talk about it in our programming and in our religious services. In fact, I spent many school breaks visiting out-of-town friends from this community. We came together through our shared interest in Judaism.

My network became bigger when I went to camp and met teens from other NFTY regions. I served on the regional board of NFTY-Southwest and then on the North American board for the organization, and **the value of building community** was the singular focus of how we would plan our events.

We also learned how not to "break" community. For example, during my first summer at camp, someone dropped a tray of plates and silverware in the dining hall, making a loud crashing noise. As sometimes is customary in these situations, everyone else in the room applauded. However, using applause to mock someone who already has drawn unwanted attention to themselves creates a "break" between the person who dropped the tray and the community, rather than building a bridge. That was a great opportunity to learn the value of community. Needless to say, mocking applause never happened at camp again.

All of this is to say that networking is happening constantly in all of these situations. Being part of a community means being a part of a network. It is completely natural to you already. If you get one thing out of this book, that's what I want it to be. Networking isn't this weird, often obnoxious thing people do self-servingly to get ahead in their professional lives. It happens every day in every way with everyone you know. It's important to make sure that when you're in these communities you are doing your part to build them, rather than break them.

You Also Harness Your Network's Power Without Realizing It

You may be thinking that merely being in a network is very different than using that network to help you achieve your goals. But is it really? Sure, being on a high school baseball team is fine, but asking your teammate to talk to his aunt because she works in a field in which you're interested is a different level of discomfort.

While you network every day by building community, you also harness your network every day without realizing it. Have you ever been in a debate with a friend and asked another person to settle it? What about asking friends for recommendations for places to eat or sites to see when traveling? Soliciting opinions is an example of harnessing the power of your network. It follows the old adage that "two heads are better than one."

Think back to those people who make their living based on word-of-mouth recommendations. It's the other side of the same coin. When people need a new service provider, the first place they go to is to their network. There are catchy terms for this, like "hive mind" for example, but it's all networking!

It's Called Social *Networking* for a Reason

Facebook. Twitter. Instagram. Snapchat. They're collectively known by two different names: "social media" and "social *networking*." Ah, there's that word again!

Yes, it's true that these sites are all about networking. That's what they were designed to do. Having accounts on these sites is not a solitary activity. You log onto your social media sites to connect with other people you know. Social networking sites have made the work of networking much easier, providing you with the capacity to keep in touch with people from your past more than ever.

I often see people use their social media accounts to effectively harness the power of their network. The best way to ask the most people for their opinion or recommendation on something is to ask on social media. You can get more responses faster than you could otherwise.

My mother has built an entire business on Facebook. She is a health coach and she uses Facebook to market her service. She posts recipes, inspirational quotes, and transformation photos of people who have lost weight and achieved optimal health using her plan. Whenever someone leaves a comment that they are interested in learning more, she always follows up with a direct message and offers to have a phone conversation. In a little over two years, she has helped hundreds of people get healthy. Some are friends from high school or college, and others are people she met online, but all of them are connected to her by her social network.

Facebook groups are great examples of online communities. High school classes, fan clubs, and other organizations that may exist offline use this feature to build community online as well. You can find communities on Facebook for virtually any interest. For example, my mom uses Facebook groups for her business, where she and all her clients can share tips, suggestions, and successes. In the past few years, millions of people have joined Facebook groups dedicated to sharing memes in a variety of contexts, including colleges, political campaigns, and everything in between. Have you ever seen a Facebook group titled, "Dank Memes for _____ Teens" or other variations? Posting memes builds community!

Talking about social networking sites merits a disclaimer of caution. Studies have proven that often, use of these sites makes people less happy and more envious of their friends' lives (at least, the way they present themselves online). People often use their networks in unhealthy ways, like obsessing over the number of "likes" their latest Instagram post garners. Plus, we have learned a lot in recent years about companies using personal data online to serve ads and how foreign countries have used social media to influence the American political process. These are big red flags that should not be ignored.

Despite these negative attributes, social media still makes networking much easier than ever. Even if you are averse to social media, you should at least consider a LinkedIn account. We'll give LinkedIn, which is like Facebook but for the professional world, a more in-depth look in a later chapter.

In any case, start to be more mindful of how you use social media and notice the ways in which you're using these sites to network. You'll surprise yourself. If you aren't on these sites, I would suggest giving them a try (with the aforementioned cautions in mind). They make networking so easy and put connecting with others right at your fingertips!

Some Harsh Realities

I hope so far that you have been convinced that networking is natural and easier than you think. Before we go any further, I want to acknowledge and confront some of the harsh realities about networking. Old-school networks like "old boys' clubs" are often rightfully derided for being exclusive, grabbing onto power and not sharing it, and creating and exacerbating divides by class, race, and gender. This is how networking is often utilized, and it's very problematic. People have used their connections to call in favors and avoid facing consequences for illegal actions. In this way, corruption is often perpetuated through networking.

In a less intense but just as inequitable way, the more socioeconomic privilege one has, the stronger and more powerful one's network will be. That's a reality, and it's highly unfair. People who are born into families that have wealth and power are much better equipped to use their networks to achieve their goals than those less privileged. They are also more likely to have more influential and well-resourced people in their networks. In another sense, less privileged people have to work harder at networking than those with more privilege.

For example, if my grandfather was Norman Lear, a pioneering television writer and producer who created a string of groundbreaking sitcoms in the 1970s, I would have a much easier time achieving my goal of working in the entertainment industry. Through my family, I would have grown up knowing the right people and they would be more likely to give me opportunities, either because they assume I must have inherited some innate skill or talent (an unreasonable assumption) or just to please my well-respected and powerful grandfather.

My grandfather is not Norman Lear. In fact, I don't have anyone in my close family in the entertainment industry. So, I'm already at a disadvantage against the children and grandchildren of producers, studio executives, agents, and celebrities. However, because I was born into a family of professionals who went to college and even have postgraduate degrees, the networks of my family members tend to be educated professionals as well. I may not have a family member in the industry, but many of my relatives know people from their networks who just so happen to be in the industry. Therefore, I've been able to grow my network through second-degree connections. Taking advantage of these connections takes some work, but the fact that they exist is due to the luck of the draw of the communities that I am a part of already.

The reality of the systemic inequities is undeniable, and it is important to recognize the privileges one has. While I have worked very hard to cultivate my network, I absolutely understand that it is much harder to do this work for many people. For people who come from less privileged backgrounds, it is not as easy to access people that they want to know. This does not change the other big reality of networking, though: it still runs the world.

It's not fair at all and working to change these kinds of systems is admirable, but change takes time. Meanwhile, those who do not harness the power of their network and work to grow it will lose out.

No matter how unfair it is, you have to play the game. If it means working harder, so be it, but no matter how privileged you may or may not be, you can utilize your current position in life to get where you want to go. The rest of this book moves past theory and will get down to brass tacks on how to actually do the work of networking. I hope this book helps you find creative ways to tap into your network so you can start to build momentum to overcome the challenges you face.

First and Foremost, Network to Learn

Up to this point, we have discussed the theory of networking and attempted to demystify and destigmatize it. Hopefully, you can see now that you already have a network based on the communities you're in, and that you are in fact networking every day.

The next step is more difficult: growing and expanding your network to include people who will help you achieve your goals. Sure, it's great to have friends from high school that you keep in touch with, but if your friends are all becoming engineers and you want to go into investment banking, they can't really help you much. You have to go beyond them to people who can. Now is the time to begin the work of creating and building a community of supportive collaborators and allies with common *professional* interests.

However, first we must answer the why. Why is it worth it to put yourself out there? Why should you make the effort to reach out to new people? There are a few reasons, but the primary one is education. First and foremost, network to learn.

Reflecting back on the discussion of the exasperated "when will I ever need to know this?" question we would ask in school, it is true that much of what we spend time learning in school won't be needed in our jobs. By contrast, there's so much information about various careers that we don't learn in school. How can we learn that? Sure, we could read about it on the

Internet, but it is not the same as getting information from someone who actually does the work.

How does one get hired to write for a show like *Game of Thrones?* How does one get to be a commentator on CNN, or work in the front office of an NBA team? Connecting with people who have achieved those goals is the best way to get insight into your chosen field.

As previously mentioned, when I was in college, I knew I wanted to work in the entertainment industry, but I didn't know how to get there. Entertainment companies, for the most part, were not visiting my campus like other industries, so readily available information was scarce. I needed to learn more myself.

I logged onto Penn's online alumni database, QuakerNet. I used to joke to fellow students that having access to the contact information of every living person who went to Penn was so valuable it was worth the cost of tuition alone. Given the astronomical rise of the cost of attending college, I don't know how long I'll be able to stand behind that statement, but I still believe that of all the benefits afforded to a person who attends a college or university, the alumni database is among the most valuable.

In the database, I searched by industry to find people who had "television" tagged on their profile and contacted them. I was able to get many of them on the phone to chat about their professional life stories. It turned out to be of vital importance that I did, because had I not, I would have been at a severe disadvantage trying to get an internship or job in Los Angeles or New York. I learned there are many different careers in the industry and the clearest path to most start at talent agencies. These companies are at the center of all the deals made in Hollywood and there are relatively few such agencies, as the majority of talent is represented by the same handful of companies. Getting a job at one means starting out in the company mailroom for several months before becoming an administrative assistant to an agent. These agencies are major companies with hundreds of employees and there are a large number of applicants vying for these limited positions. Because they deal mainly within the entertainment industry, these companies are not household names. I would have not known anything about the talent agencies had I not reached out to alumni in the industry.

We will cover the details of how to reach out and make these connections in depth, but it is important not to get too far ahead of yourself. Yes, you want a job and you want help getting one, but it is even more important to take the time to learn about it. Networking is the best way to do that. Yes, it is what you know, and it is who you know, but most importantly, it's what you know *from* who you know that counts.

How to Find People You Want to Know

Now comes the fun part. You have a network already, but now you're looking to expand it to include people you want to know. There are people who can teach you and help you achieve your goals. How do you find those people? It's time to get creative.

Be Clear About Your Goals

You'll be surprised how much your existing network will want to help you connect with the right people to reach your goals. When you care about a member of your community, you want to help them succeed. Remember our working definition of networking? You just have to help your network help you by clearly articulating your goals.

What are you interested in doing? What do you want to know more about? Being able to specifically articulate your goals will help you be connected to the right contacts. People are very busy (including you!) so it is important not to waste everyone's time by being connected to someone only tangentially related to what you want to do. For example, when I was interested in being connected to those in the entertainment industry, I was given the opportunity to speak to a marketing director in the home video division of a studio. I was more interested in writing and creative development for television, so I did not pursue this particular opportunity.

There's some natural and totally valid pushback to this. Why wouldn't you take every opportunity you can get? You never know, your interests might change! You could still learn something valuable! These are all good points. Maybe I should have taken the opportunity to speak to the marketing director. It is still important to be able to articulate what you want while being open to new possibilities. As you continue on your networking journey, you will be able to better define and refine your goals and home in more narrowly on the people from whom you can best learn.

Your Network's Networks

It's been alluded to already, but it's important to focus on the best place to start: your network's networks.

Think about all the people you know already: your family, friends, classmates from school, coworkers, etc. Each one of these people have networks of their own. They have their own families, friends, old classmates, and on and on. This is the best place to start expanding your network! Your friend's cousin or your cousin's friend could be the key that unlocks the next door on your journey. Tap into those networks. It is a small world after all, and you'll be surprised who knows whom. I guarantee you they'll be happy to connect you.

We are lucky to live in the digital age because we have Facebook, which does a great job helping us visualize these ever-intersecting networks. You can see who your mutual friends are with everyone. The same is true for LinkedIn. In fact, there is a feature on LinkedIn that allows you to ask a mutual connection with someone for an introduction. Facebook and LinkedIn reflect the way networks work in real life as well. Between you and another person, there could be a few intersecting points: your mutual friends.

I often say that one of my favorite parts of being Jewish is the concept of "Jewish Geography." Urban Dictionary defines it as "when two or more Jews get together and discuss who knows whose Jewish friends and relatives from where." It feels sometimes like all Jews are connected, and especially with Jewish youth groups and camps and large families in general, the game of Jewish geography gets played often and connections are often found. It's like the original version of Facebook mutual friends, and there are so many fun examples.

In high school, for instance, I attended a Tuesday night "Hebrew High" at the Jewish community center, which was taught by an *extremely* well-connected person in the greater Phoenix Jewish community. As an icebreaker on the first day, the class of about 25 teens introduced themselves to everyone. If the teacher knew the person's family, she followed up by revealing the connection. She knew about 90% of us, including myself, as her husband is a distant relative of my dad.

In another example, my mother grew up in a small Jewish community in Alabama, then attended a large university in Texas, where she joined a Jewish sorority, before living in Dallas, then Phoenix. She now feels like she has a connection to every Jewish person around her age in the south. Whenever she meets a new southern Jew, she'll always try to find mutual connections with them, and it often works.

Because I spent so much time in Jewish teen leadership on the North American level in high school, whenever I meet a Jewish person about my age from virtually anywhere, I try to play Jewish Geography with them. Often, we just pull out our phones and head straight to Facebook to tell us who are our mutual friends (a lazy version of Jewish Geography), and there's often a connection.

I have heard people from other ethnic and cultural backgrounds say there is a similar Jewish Geography-esque concept in their communities as well. Capitalize on it! Investigate these second-degree connections, wherever they come from, and see where they lead.

Get Your Connections to Connect You and Take It from There

When making a connection with someone you don't know, sometimes you're not sure if they are willing to chat with you or not. They could be a very busy and important person who just may not have the time. Sometimes, someone I know will say to me, "Oh I know _____, you should contact her and tell her I sent you." I always ask our mutual connection if instead they will reach out and make sure that it is okay that I contact them. It always is, but I don't like to surprise people. It would be awkward to reach out to someone who is not open to connecting with me, and then have to let our mutual friend know about the failed connection.

Sometimes, the mutual connection will even go the extra step of making a formal introduction via email. That's very nice, but not necessary. Remember, these connections are *favors* people are doing for you. No one has to connect you with their friend or relative, but they are doing so because they like and care about you and want to help you succeed. Show your appreciation by minimizing the work they have to do on their end. Yes, I like to have them reach out to the person to make sure they're willing to talk with me, but I always take it from there and do the legwork myself.

Always take initiative. If this kind of second-degree connection comes up, never wait for that person to reach out to you. If it is something you want to pursue, it is always incumbent upon you to be proactive and make it happen.

College Alumni

Another way to find potential connections is from your college alumni directory. I've mentioned already how I utilized mine to reach out to people in the entertainment industry, and it really was a tremendous resource.

Having gone to the same college or university as another person counts as a common interest, creating a community of alumni. Often, when alumni hear from current students or younger alumni wanting to talk to them about their careers, they are very willing to help out a fellow Quaker, Wildcat, or Gator. It's a bond and a great icebreaker. They are flattered when a student reaches out. They see themselves in you because they used to be in your place and want to help the next generation.

I first started reaching out to alumni when I was looking to get an internship after my sophomore year of college. I was interested in TV studios and networks but didn't really know what else was out there. One alumnus I spoke to was just a few years older than me and was a showrunner's assistant at a sketch comedy show. He suggested I look into his boss's management company. It turns out in addition to agencies, there are companies full of people who "manage" the careers of talent. Some of these companies don't even have websites because they only deal with their famous clients and don't care to be found by the outside world. I got an internship at the management company mentioned by the alumnus and I had an amazing summer. I made lots of friends who I keep in touch with and one of them became my roommate when I first moved to Los Angeles after college. I would have never even heard of this company were it not for that alumni connection.

When I was on the Wharton Undergraduate Media and Entertainment Club board and would coach other students on how to network, they would sometimes complain to me that they have no existing connections in the industry. I told them our alumni database is the great equalizer. It doesn't matter what your background is. Everyone at school has the same access to the same alumni network. The ones who get ahead will be the ones who utilize it.

If you go to or went to a college or university, the same applies to you. You should have access to an alumni database with contact information for everyone who went to your school. Hopefully, there will be a way to search by other criteria such as industry, company, or city. LinkedIn also has a feature to help college alumni connect. If you need help with this, reach out to your school's alumni association or career center. I'm sure they'd be more than happy to help you navigate alumni resources.

Speaker/Panel Events

Another way to find people you want to know are at speaker or panel events about topics of interest to you. Quite often, these happen in academic settings, so it is much easier to find and attend these events as a student, but they are everywhere! At my school, various diplomats, media personalities, and politicians often came to speak or participate on panels on various topics, usually in policy. My political friends interested in these topics would always make sure to go to these panels.

If you find yourself in the audience of one of these events, there are a few ways you can stand out from the crowd and make a lasting impression with the speaker or panelist. First, come prepared with thoughtful, insightful questions to ask. If there's time at the end of the presentation for questions, you'll most likely only get to ask just one. Sometimes, at the end of the formal portion of the event, you can approach the panelist or speaker personally. If it is a really important person, like a senator, this may not be possible, so it's important to gauge the situation.

In the appropriate setting, when you approach a speaker, make sure to thank them for their time and let them know you learned a lot. Be specific about what really struck you so they know they had an impact. This would be another opportunity to ask another insightful question. Now again, it all depends on the situation, but often the contact information for these speakers becomes available at the event. Maybe their email address shows up in the slideshow presentation. Maybe you can somehow obtain a business card. Maybe with *very light* investigating online, you can find their email address (very light being the operative phrase, because you don't want to come off as creepy! If it's readily available on a website that anyone can find, no big deal. If you have to do a lot of snooping, they probably are not trying to make themselves available to be contacted).

It's important to *follow up* within 24 hours to thank them again and make sure they remember who you are. If you asked a question at the event, working that into your email helps jog their memory. If not, use it to reiterate specifically what you enjoyed most. Often, they will respond with something nice (albeit usually way shorter and less formal than what you will write) thanking you for the kind words and possibly an offer to keep in touch.

Random Encounters and Business Cards

You could also get lucky and randomly meet someone who would be an asset to your network! Sitting next to someone on an airplane, waiting in line behind someone, or other chance encounters are very memorable ways of meeting! In such situations, people often exchange business cards as a way to stay in touch.

If such a chance encounter happens to you and you walk away with a business card of a new contact, *always* follow up within 24 hours with a similar message described in the previous section. Let them know it was nice to meet them, say something specific about your encounter that you particularly enjoyed, and suggest keeping in touch. Also, you do not want to lose the information on the card! Keeping the card itself is not as big a deal (although it can be fun to have a business card collection), but you should have a way to keep the contact information organized.

There's nothing wrong with creating a new contact in your phone for the person, even if you won't be connecting with them often. There are business card apps, like CamCard, where you can use your smart phone to take a photo of the card and the app stores all the information. It creates its own contact list for the business cards you've collected. Spreadsheets are always good for this sort of information as well.

Summary

If you're looking to expand your network, there are a few ways to start. Look to your immediate network and see if you can tap into their networks. If you are connected to a college or university, utilize their alumni resources. Anyone you come across at a speaker or panel event could be an important contact as well. In any circumstance you receive someone else's business card, make sure to keep track of the information and follow up on it.

All of this means being proactive and maybe stepping out of your comfort zone. After all, it can be awkward and uncomfortable to reach out to new people. If you're willing to do this, you're already a step ahead of the curve. Many people let the discomfort win and they avoid it altogether. Look at all the connections those people miss out on! If you've made it this far, you're doing great!

How to Reach Out

Now you have some new people you want to know. You've talked to your own network or you've scoured your college alumni database and now you want to reach out and make the connection. This is the exciting part! These people may be strangers, but soon they won't be if you do it the right way. The objective here is to *get a response*. It feels really awful when you put yourself out there to a new person and you feel rejected by way of being ignored. Therefore, it is important to reach out in a way that will maximize the chance they reply. You can do this with a cold email.

A cold email, like a cold call, is an unsolicited and unprompted overture from one person to another, often a stranger. People cold call typically in an attempt to sell something, but you are not selling anything here. In fact, you really have nothing to offer at all. You're asking for something.

What You Can and Can't Ask For

In a cold email, you are limited in what you can ask since you don't know the recipient at all. They may be nice and generous with their time, but people don't really have the time to go far out of their way for a relative stranger, so the ask has to be a small, reasonable one.

You **cannot**, I repeat, **cannot**, ask them to do you a favor or directly help you achieve your goal right off the bat. That goes against the entire philosophy of networking this book has described so far. Can you imagine if you were a busy working person and you got an email from some kid who goes to your college asking if you can get them an internship or job at your company? What would you do? You'd delete that email and never respond, because that's self-serving and obnoxious. It also the violates the "network to learn" principle. Are you really going to take the time and effort to reach out to a new person in a field you're interested in, make no attempt to learn from them, and instead ask them to do you a favor? No!

This doesn't mean that you can *never* ask for a favor. Eventually, you'll use your network to help you achieve your goals and you'll help achieve other people's goals, but you can't start out that way. You have to do the work of building those relationships first.

What you can ask for is information. You can (and should) ask for a few minutes of their time to chat with you about themselves, their career, and their industry. It's called an **informational interview,** and it's exactly what it sounds like. It's a chance for you to ask them questions and for you to learn. The benefit is all for you, and it's a generous gift of time from them, but it's not a big ask.

People love talking about themselves, so they will probably agree to chat if you have a mutual connection or you went to the same college. They will be more than happy to take a few minutes out of their day to impart their wisdom. It makes them feel important and validated! Imagine you're a busy person and instead of getting a cold email from a stranger asking for a favor, you get an earnest email from someone wanting to learn from you. You'd definitely say yes to that! I'm grateful to Penn Career Services for teaching me about informational interviews.

How to Cold Email

In order to maximize your chances of getting a response to your cold email, you have to make sure, first and foremost, that it is relatively short and sweet. Busy people do not write long, flowery emails and do not want to take the time to read them either. You want to be clear and concise about who you are, how you got their name and email, why you are reaching out, and what you are looking for from them.

Most people will only spend a few seconds reading an email, so you want to make sure you capture their attention early on and keep it long enough to get them to complete your ask for an informational interview. The way you capture their attention is with the subject line of the email, something I learned from a great networking book called *Coffee Lunch Coffee* by Alana Muller.

As an aside, this book was something I was introduced to through my network, as Alana is a family friend of my uncle's best friend from college. I heard about her book from talking to my uncle's friend at a family event. It was so cool to be able to use the skills I learned from her book to write her an email letting her know how much I enjoyed it.

But back to subject lines. Many people delete emails without even opening them if they think it is junk or otherwise unimportant. You want to make sure that upon reading the subject line they deem it important enough to open.

If you are reaching out to someone you were connected to by a mutual friend, you should include your mutual connection's name in the subject line. If I was your connection to the recipient, the subject line should read, "Introduction by Scott Rubenstein." With your mutual friend's name included, the contact knows you aren't just some rando and they'll be much more likely to open the email and respond. Hopefully they were expecting to hear from you anyway since your mutual connection asked them for their permission first for you to reach out.

For college alumni, you should include the fact that you're a student at their alma mater in your subject line, and, in this case, let them know what you are asking for in a few words. This is not as necessary when you already have a mutual connection like in the first example, because hopefully they'll be expecting your email. An alumni email will truly be a cold one. You could maybe use "informational interview" in the subject line, but that could sound a little too formal and it's possible they won't recognize the term. I like to use the phrase "career guidance questions," which is basically the definition of an informational interview. The emails I send would have the subject line, "Penn student—career guidance questions."

If you are following up from meeting them organically or seeing them speak on a panel, make sure you note that in the subject line. It can be something like "Follow up from _____," or "Nice to meet you at _____" to remind them they met you already.

After capturing their attention with a subject line, write a nice, concise email explaining who you are and why you're reaching out. Then, you'll end with the ask: the informational interview. You want to make sure that you're specific in what you're looking for while also giving a few different options to them for how to proceed.

If you're in the same city, you can propose meeting in person in a variety of settings, depending on the situation. You can offer to visit them at their office or to meet over coffee, drinks, or a meal. It depends on who the person is and what they do. For example, if they are much older and are a partner at a law firm, I'd probably suggest an office visit. If they are not much older than you and they may not have an office big enough for you to visit, meeting outside of work over a coffee might be more appropriate. Give them options! Let them know that you are flexible, grateful for their time, and willing to accommodate them. Be sure to offer a phone call as an option as well. Meeting in person is always best because you can really get to know each other and it's more memorable, but some people are too busy for that and can only hop on the phone. That's okay as well! Of course, if you are not in the same city, it is going to be a phone call. Make sure when you're making the arrangements, you know who is calling whom. Remember, they are doing *you* a favor just by talking to you.

In terms of timing, make sure to offer them reasonable timeframes in order to maximize the chance of getting a yes. When you're making your ask, give them a timeframe that they can commit to easily; 15 to 20 minutes is a good range. Asking for any more time is too big of a favor. Some people would say you should ask for something even shorter, like 5 to 10 minutes. That's okay as well. I tend to shoot for 15 to 20 because it seems more likely. People know they won't just be on the phone or especially in an in-person meeting for only a few minutes. Most of my informational interviews last longer than 20 minutes, so it's not essential that you actually stick to the timeframe if the conversation is flowing easily. Remember, the goal is to get them to agree to talk. I ask if they have time "in the next few weeks" so it gives them flexibility, but it also lets them know that I am eager to talk with them. If you don't indicate you'd like to speak soon, they may forget about it or it'll never get scheduled in the first place. Giving them an open time frame but letting them know you're excited about speaking to them is the best way to frame your intentions.

To reiterate, give them options, but be clear about what you want. You can't expect them to read your mind.

Recently, I was coaching a friend on how to follow up with a speaker she saw at an event. She said, "Maybe I'll just email him and say I'm interested in learning more about what he has to say and hope he offers to get coffee." I told her that if she truly wants to have coffee with him, she needs to let him know! He can't read her mind. Be flexible about the time, place, and method of conversation, but *ask* for what you want. People are busy; they don't have time to figure you out.

So, putting it all together, here's an example of an email I would write to an alumnus of my school that I found on our alumni database:

Subject: Penn Student—career guidance questions

Hi Mr. Smith,

My name is Scott Rubenstein and I'm a sophomore at Penn studying Communication. I came across your information via a search through Penn's alumni database, QuakerNet. My ultimate goal is to work in scripted television, but more immediately I am looking for an internship in the industry for this summer. I see from your QuakerNet profile that you worked for CBS and 20th Century Fox and wrote for *The Office* (one of my favorite shows)! If you have about 20 minutes to spare in the next few weeks, I'd really appreciate the chance to hop on the phone and ask you a few questions about how you made it from Penn to the TV industry. I would love to learn from your experiences.

I look forward to hearing from you!

Sincerely,

Scott Rubenstein

Notice that I'm not being shy about letting him know that I'm looking for work in the entertainment industry. I'm just not asking him to help me find something. I'm asking for information. He knows that I want to get an internship, but hopefully he'll know that I'm also serious about learning from him, because that's what my ask is. It doesn't hurt to mention my goals so it's in the back of his mind, but reaching out cold and asking for a favor requiring effort for him is a turnoff.

Trying Again and Giving Up

A career advisor at my school said that when you send out these types of cold emails to alumni, the response rate will only be about 20%. So, if you're serious about connecting, you will need to send out a lot of these emails knowing that you won't hear back from most of them. It also underscores the importance of the technique. It's already hard enough to get them to respond. You have to communicate in such a way that will maximize your chances.

The situation is a little different if you're approaching a mutual connection (think those "Intro by ____" emails). It is much more likely that the person will reply to you in that situation, but people are still busy and can easily forget to respond and, quite frankly, you are not a priority.

So, what happens if you don't get a response? Remember the value of assuming goodwill. Don't take it personally. Assume they meant to respond, but returning your email got bogged down in their to-do list and they forgot.

It is not a bother to give them a gentle reminder. In fact, they'll most likely appreciate it and will thank you. If a week goes by and you don't hear back, feel free to forward your email to them again and say something nice like, "Hey, just want to follow up and make sure you got my email below. Looking forward to hearing from you!" It's totally appropriate—and even a good thing to do—because it shows your passion and your persistence. It can be hard to keep up with everything, and people appreciate the gentle nudge to help them out. I can't tell you how many times this has happened to me, both from new people and from people I've already known for years!

Of course, there's a fine line between a gentle reminder and downright harassment. A week is the absolute earliest you can follow up. If you don't hear from them after the second time, that means it is time to give up. You tried your best, but they're just too busy. It's time to move on to the next person.

Yes, there's a bit of an art form to reaching out, but once you get the hang of it, it won't feel awkward. It will begin to feel more natural. It really is a great way for young people to make new connections and learn from experienced people.

The Informational Interview

You've done it! You've made a new connection with a new person by securing an informational interview. This is where the magic happens. This is your place to learn and it's also your place to shine. Even though it may sound cliché, they're interviewing you just as much as you're interviewing them. While you talk to them, they are trying to figure out if you are an interesting and dynamic person that they will want to continue to know and help in the future. They want to know if you are worth being in their network! You have to prove that you are.

Preparation

You should prepare properly in advance of your informational interview. If possible, familiarize yourself with the background of the person with whom you'll be speaking. A light Google search may accomplish this mission. You don't have to act like an FBI investigator. Also, it's not necessary to prove to them that you prepared. For example, if you find out where they got their law degree, you don't have to say, "I know you got your JD from the University of Virginia," because that may come off as a little creepy. Just familiarize yourself with the basics of what they have done in their career and use it as a springboard to ask them questions.

For example, "I know you used to work in tech before moving over to baseball administration, what was that transition like?" is a great question to ask. It shows you're somewhat familiar with them and have done your research, but you haven't stalked them.

Also, until you are good at conducting informational interviews, you should write down about five questions that you want to ask in advance to make sure you know how you want the conversation to go. Sometimes, these talks can be awkward at first, so having this list will help you avoid weird silences.

It's very possible that your conversation will take a different direction than you planned, leading you to new questions you hadn't considered. That's amazing! Go with it! It's not crucial that all the questions you wrote down are answered. Ask the important ones at the beginning to make sure you get to them. You don't want to keep the person longer than they are comfortable, so skip your less important questions. You'll hopefully be able to gauge their time constraint by social cues.

I have done over 50 of these informational interviews throughout college and beyond, and they really become second nature as you keep doing them. Soon you won't need to write any questions out in advance. You'll know exactly what you want to say and how you'll proceed. However, it's still important to have notetaking capabilities at the ready! I have a specific legal pad that I use for informational interviews. I scribble notes all over the page! I write down any kernels of wisdom I hear, both so I can remember and also so I can refer to them later in my thank-you note. I also write down their background information. When you do a lot of informational interviews, it can be hard to differentiate between everyone's backstories. It's best to take notes.

Keep the Spotlight on Them

This is an informational interview of *them*. They'll hopefully want to know about you, your interests, and what led you to them, but don't monopolize the conversation by talking about yourself too much. Make sure the bulk of the time is spent talking about them and their career. You can ask their opinion on current events in the field or other relevant matters as well. It should definitely be a conversation, with you responding to what they say and asking follow-up questions where appropriate, but keep the focus on them.

What should you be asking in an informational interview? There are two broad areas of focus:

1) How they got to where they are today
2) What they currently do in their job/what their job is like

These two areas should get a person talking for several minutes at the very least. Depending on how experienced they are, they may have a lot to say to fill in these two topics. They may say quite a few things on which you'll want to follow up with more questions. Write them down so you don't forget!

Hopefully, their story will be very illuminating for you. I know for me, it was really helpful hearing how people went from college to where they are today in the entertainment industry. There's no one set path, and learning about different journeys was very informative. You should be able to get a lot of information from those two areas. Of course, any other relevant questions about the field of interest or anything else is fair game as well! Make sure you ask the questions at an appropriate time in the conversation without interrupting their flow of thought.

How to End the Interview

You've had a great informational interview and you've learned a lot from this person. You may even feel like you've connected with them on a personal level and enjoy their company. That's amazing! You've had a successful interaction. Finishing it up well and sticking the landing are really important to sealing the deal. When the time comes to wrap up your conversation, there are a few important things to keep in mind.

First, if you say at the beginning of the interaction that you are looking for a job or an internship, it is very likely that they may offer to help you if they can. By the end of the conversation, hopefully you will have impressed them enough that they will want to help you.

Think back to the definition of networking! It's a community of supportive collaborators and *allies*. By reaching out and asking someone about themselves, you're moving from stranger territory to potential ally territory. As mentioned, people love to talk about themselves, and they'll think that you are intellectually inquisitive, interesting, and nice enough to warrant their help (good judgment on their part, you totally are)! If they don't offer that help, you *still* can't ask for it yet, but know that if you maintain the connection beyond this conversation, they may offer in the future.

There is one thing you can ask them for though, and that's more connections! Why not take this opportunity to expand your network even further, get more interesting stories and perspectives, and generally learn more? At the end of the conversation, ask them if they know anyone else who they think might be willing to talk to you. This is a simple ask of them. They are not "pulling strings" for you per se, they're just connecting you to another nice person who is generous with their time and willing to talk about themselves with you. The answer is not always yes to this question. Sometimes people will honestly tell me that they don't have anyone to connect me with, and that's okay. Ask them to let you know if they think of anyone after your conversation. If they say they have a new connection for you, make sure you follow up to get their contact information so you can reach out!

Most importantly, you should make sure that the end of your conversation leaves the door open for a further relationship. Networking is about developing relationships over time. You don't want this to be a one-and-done. Be sure to articulate that to them. Let them know you want to continue to keep in touch. They will probably agree to leave the door open and offer for you to follow up with them if you have any more questions. Take them up on it (more on following up a little later). Of course, you will thank them for talking to you in person or while on the call, but there's still more thanking to do.

The Thank-You

The thank-you is about as important as the entire informational interview experience itself, so make sure you always send a thank-you note. Even though it should be a given, many people don't send one. If you do send a thank-you note, you'll stand out from the pack, especially if you write a genuine, thoughtful one.

My mom drilled in the importance of thank-you notes to me from a very young age. I can't remember how old I was, but I do remember that I was writing thank-you notes for birthday presents earlier than my peers. For young children, they make fill-in-the-blank thank-you notes. I did not spend much time writing those before I graduated into the fully handwritten ones. I distinctly remember going to a birthday party around the age of 7 years old when, after the gifts were opened, relatives of the birthday boy quickly wrote fill-in-the-blank thank-you notes for all the gifts and slid them into the party favors before parents came to pick up their kids. My mom disapproved and made sure I knew how important it was to write my own thank-you notes. Her feelings did not change over the years, even when I had to write 200 thank-you notes after my Bar Mitzvah!

Obviously, the purpose of the thank-you note should not be self-serving; *however*, there's nothing wrong with using the opportunity to make a good impression one last time. If you wow them with a really thoughtful thank-you note, it can go a long way. It even may be the one takeaway your new contact will remember about you.

To hearken back to an earlier section, it is important that your thank-you note be specific about what you appreciated. It shows that you were listening and also lets them know what kind of an impact they had on you. It gives them a sense of how you think and what your focus was in the context of the conversation. It may help them to better help you in the future.

Ideally, the thank-you note should be sent within 24 hours of your meeting. It is very important that it happen within this timeframe in order to keep the momentum and show your appreciation earnestly. If you wait too much longer than this window of time, it may seem like an afterthought.

If you can, send a handwritten thank-you note. Making this effort will show your true appreciation and again separate you from most of your counterparts. In the digital age, people are still very excited to receive mail. It will make their day even more than an email that can get lost easily. With a handwritten note, they would also have a physical item they associate with you, so they'll remember you better.

This is not to say that a thank-you email would not suffice. As long as it is genuine, heartfelt, and well-written, a thank-you email can have almost the same effect. If you were set up by a mutual friend, ask your friend for your new contact's address. If you know where they work, send it to their office, but if you have to ask the intended recipient where to send a thank you note, it can be awkward. At that point, it's easier to just send the email.

Here's an example of a thank-you note that I sent after meeting someone for the first time for an informational interview:

Hey John (now since you know them, you can use their first name if appropriate!),

I just want to thank you so much for taking the time to speak with me yesterday. Hearing from an actual staff writer on a network show was definitely helpful in learning more about the business and a nice reassurance that I'm on the right track, at least for now. It was particularly illuminating to hear how you made the transition from your first job at the agency to becoming a writer's assistant. I think it will be really helpful in determining how to position myself well at my first job to get my second job.

Thank you once again, and we shall be in touch!

Best,
Scott Rubenstein

Assistants

Depending on who you are talking to, they may have an administrative assistant or scheduler that helped arrange your conversation. In the entertainment industry, I deal with assistants quite often (I am one too!). It's a tireless, often thankless job, so you will *really* stand out if you take the time to thank them too.

Be nice to assistants in general! They are the gatekeepers of their bosses and if they like you, they can help you get access in the future. Also, in many industries, being an assistant is a stepping stone to becoming the next boss. The assistants will definitely be people you will want to know in the future.

If I had a meeting with someone who has an assistant, I always email them a little note to thank them for their help arranging the meeting and to let them know that I had a nice time chatting with their boss. I bet they don't get too many of those kinds of notes, and it will *really* go a long way!

Follow-Through and Follow-Up Are Everything

Follow-through and follow-up are crucial to successful networking, and they are tied together. Follow-through means keeping your commitments, and follow-up is communicating that you have followed through. Following up is also about making sure *others* are following through on their commitments to you! Follow-through is a skill that most people need to improve. I've come to expect people not to follow through. I am surprised when they actually do follow through on what they say they will do, which is sad!

It may sound like I'm violating my principle of assuming goodwill here, but I promise I am not. I don't think people are intentional when they don't follow through. I assume it slipped through the cracks because maybe they didn't write it down and forgot. I know people are well intentioned and want to follow through on the things they say they will do, but it's disheartening how often follow-through doesn't occur. If you follow through on commitments, you'll stand out.

I once had an internship at a major TV and film corporation in a division that dealt with unscripted cable TV. The internship program encouraged us to reach out to employees for informational interviews. I was able to speak to a high-level executive in network TV development who also happened to be an alumna of my college. We had such a great conversation that I told her I wanted to bring her to Penn to speak to the Wharton

Undergraduate Media and Entertainment Club and promised to follow through on it. Although I was unable to arrange an in-person visit, we had a nice Q&A on FaceTime with her several months later. She told me she was very impressed that I followed through and made it happen. She remains a cherished mentor.

Following up can be, for example, reaching out to ask a question you thought of after you left the informational interview. This is great especially if they say you can follow up with more questions. Do it! Following up can mean letting them know you took their advice on something, even if it's small. In the entertainment industry, many conversations revolve around what content is currently out there in film and on TV. There's a lot of trading "what are you watching right now?" questions. If I get a recommendation of a TV show I'd enjoy, I try to follow through by watching it and then follow up to let the recommender know I took their advice and I appreciated the suggestion. Even if it sounds like a "throwaway line," you should still follow up. If someone says, "let me know how it goes," for example, they may just be saying that to be nice but not actually expect that you will follow up. Do it anyway! It gives you an excuse to continue to keep in touch with them, and they will be happy to hear from you.

Personally, I find it very satisfying when I recommend a TV show, book, or another piece of media to someone and they take my suggestion and enjoy it. Imagine you meet a really cool person through networking and they recommend you read a particular book to help you learn more about a topic of interest to you. Don't you think it would make their day if you email them after you've finished the book to thank them for their recommendation and explain what in particular you learned or enjoyed from it? This is another opportunity for your new contact to get to know you too. They'll learn a lot about you from the way you respond to their recommendations.

The bottom line here is to take every opportunity to follow up and don't let things slip through the cracks by not following through on action items. You'll develop a reputation as a reliable, responsible, organized person, and that will help you achieve success. Because many people don't follow through or follow up, you'll be going the extra mile if you do both, and you'll be remembered.

Afterward—Keeping in Touch

You've had your informational interview, you've sent your thank-you note, and you've followed up on any outstanding items from the conversation. You officially have a new connection in your network, but the work doesn't stop there.

If your new connection is busy, they will most likely not reach out to you themselves. If you want to maintain a relationship with them, it is incumbent upon you to reach out to them. This is a hallmark of networking at a young age, and it's especially true if your new connection is older and well-established in their career. You just won't be top-of-mind. Moreover, they might even forget about you if you do not keep the connection alive.

There are a few different ways you can stay on someone's radar. The first, as mentioned, is following up on something you discussed. Did they make a recommendation? Take it and let them know how it went. Another way a lot of my friends like to keep in touch is by sending articles to their contacts. If you see something online that you think your contact will find interesting, you can send them a link with a short note explaining why you thought of them. I have a friend from college who is also interested in the entertainment industry, and he practices this with trade publications. If a story is published in *Deadline, Variety,* or *The Hollywood Reporter* that involves someone he knows or even the company at which they work, he will send them a note with a link congratulating them on their upcoming project or deal. This can be overbearing if overdone though, so if you want to send articles to your contacts, do so sparingly!

The holidays can be a great time to reach out to contacts! Does your family send out and/or receive holiday cards every year? Receiving one means you are a valued part of the sender's community. Take this opportunity to reach out to your network! You don't have to have formal cards printed and mailed, but you can certainly send an email wishing them happy holidays.

Using Social Media

We've discussed social networking sites in an earlier chapter, but it is important to revisit them when discussing strategies for keeping in touch with new contacts. Again, it depends on the context of how you met the person and who they are, but using social media to keep in touch is highly encouraged!

Of course, there are different outlets used for different purposes. You wouldn't add your internship boss on Snapchat (well, maybe you would, who knows these days). The point is that there are levels of intimacy associated with various social networking sites.

There are people who I met through my school's alumni database who graduated only a few years before me, which puts them in my general age group. I am friends with many of these people on Facebook. There are others, like the executive who I brought to speak at school, that I don't think would be appropriate to be friends with on Facebook. The nature of our relationship is more professional.

Luckily, there is a social media site for professionals, and it's called LinkedIn. If you are not already on LinkedIn, you should create an account as soon as possible. A LinkedIn profile is basically an expanded version of one's resume, and therefore is a place to learn about someone's background. It's a great way to be connected to contacts and you can stay current with their professional lives.

LinkedIn also has a messaging feature which is great for corresponding, especially if you do not have someone's email address. It is perfectly appropriate to message just about anyone you know via LinkedIn. As mentioned, there is also an alumni search mechanism that functions similarly to an internal database your school might have. Don't forget about that introduction feature, where if you want to be connected to someone on LinkedIn, you can ask a mutual connection to make the introduction. It really is a networker's dream come true!

It is important to note that LinkedIn can tell you when other people view your profile. The browsing abilities of Facebook and Instagram are not quite as private on LinkedIn. If you have a free account, you will merely receive a notification that someone looked at your information, but you won't know their identity. So, don't shy away from that! Who cares if they get a notification saying someone looked at their profile? Do it anyway. You can only see more specific information about who is viewing your profile with a LinkedIn Premium account. From my experience, most people I know don't have a premium account, so don't let this keep you away from researching people!

If you are a member of a generation that grew up with social media, you will probably have an instinct for what is appropriate and what is not. You should use social media cautiously, and every situation is different, but the takeaway here is that LinkedIn is a great resource that makes networking easier. Use it to connect with most everyone!

The Art of Keeping in Touch

Not keeping in touch at all is bad, but so is keeping in touch too much. It's a delicate balancing act. If you overdo it, you will come off as annoying, needy, self-serving, and even socially inept. No one wants to be hounded by contacts. You should never get to the point where your name pops up in someone's inbox and they think to themselves, "Oh no, not this person again!"

There's no formula to it. I can't tell you exactly how many times per month or per year you should reach out and exactly how to space it out. I would not send an article every single week to a contact who may be a busy executive. I wouldn't even do it every month. Maybe I would reach out more often to a different contact. It's something that you'll hopefully figure out as you go along. You'll be able to develop a sense of what is appropriate.

By the way, if you reach out to a contact and they don't respond, use your follow-up cautiously as well! This is not the same situation as asking for an informational interview and then following up a week later if there's no response. If you send an "I'm thinking of you" note with an article and they don't respond, do not follow up a week later with a "did you see my note?" You're not really asking anything of them in this type of correspondence, so the expectation they reply is not as high. Let it go and reach out again when an appropriate amount of time has passed.

These are the types of situations that will begin to come naturally to you as you network more. You'll soon realize that professional networking is similar to interactions with people you're far more comfortable with, like family and friends. Without thinking too much about it, you'll be able to discern how to most appropriately behave toward the different people who fill different roles in your life. Keeping in touch may be an art form, but it's one anyone can pick up easily.

It can really pay off as well. One of the people I have kept in touch with is an alumnus from my college with whom I had an informational interview over the phone. I made sure to meet up in person with him the following two summers when I was in Los Angeles. He told me that he was very impressed that I had kept in touch so long, and that he speaks to quite a few students from Penn and no one makes the effort to keep in touch. We're on a texting basis now, and I have a feeling we may grow even closer now that I live in Los Angeles. You'll stand out if you make the effort. It's worth it!

When Can I Start Asking for Favors?

You've worked so hard to cultivate your network. You've been connected by family and friends, you've cold emailed, you've had informational interviews, you've thanked them, you've done all the appropriate follow-ups. You've known your new connection for months, maybe even years. You really want a job at their company or somewhere they may have contacts. A recommendation or a referral from them would go a long way in cutting through the mountains of resumes a company receives. You think that they would be willing to give you a boost. Can you ask them?

Yes! They're part of your network, your community of supportive collaborators and allies who share common interests and who desire to share in *your* success. What does that really boil down to? You've developed a relationship! They *care* about you, and because of that, they want to help you. By now, I hope you care about them too.

Think back to the chapter about cold emailing and reaching out to new contacts. What if instead of doing the informational interview, learning from them, following up and keeping in touch, you skipped all that and just asked them for a favor? Would they have cared about you at that point? No! This is why networking is about building relationships and community. It takes time, care, and effort.

I'm thinking in years. If you want to build a community of supportive collaborators and allies, you should start that work long before you will really need to lean on them. There are Penn alumni I have still not asked for a favor, even though we connected when I was a sophomore in college. It's been years now, and every time I have been in Los Angeles since our initial informational interview, I have reached out to get together and catch up. You'll be more successful in building that community of allies if you put in the work over a long period of time.

I hope you've seen that asking for favors is not the only reason why you should have a network and there are many other benefits to these relationships. This isn't to say that you should avoid asking for favors. Everyone needs help from others and as we've established, the world runs on networking. Don't be shy about asking for help when you need it.

Honestly, it is more likely your favor will be granted if you put in the time and effort over the long haul. It's a lot like saving money, but instead of cash, you're saving "social currency." There's a huge difference between seeking assistance after you've built up this social currency over time and just trying to get a stranger to help you because they went to your college. Think of it this way: if you don't care about them, they won't care about you. If the roles were reversed, would you help them out if they asked you? If so, that's a good indicator you've built up enough social currency that you can afford to spend a little on a favor.

Sometimes You Don't Have to Ask

It's been alluded to already, but sometimes in that very first interaction, your new contact may offer to help you without you asking. That's great! Feel free to take them up on it. They're offering! You'll notice, however, that they will make that offer at the end of the conversation, after they've gotten to know you a bit and decided they like you. It's still not the same as the idea of you reaching out to them as a stranger and asking for a favor. It's about building up the goodwill (another word for social currency!) so they care about you and want to help you. Sometimes, that goodwill can be built up over the course of one conversation, but it is incumbent upon your new contact to determine if that's the case and offer you something.

The Asks Are Still Small

Even if you are comfortable making an ask, it should still be a small one. Can someone send a short email on your behalf? Maybe a quick phone call? Contacts are usually good at getting you interviews, but not a job itself. You still have to do that on your own. Don't expect too much from contacts. Most of the places I applied for my first job in the entertainment industry would probably not even reach out and grant me an interview without a nudge from a contact. That's the kind of work your network can do. They usually cannot move mountains and place you in a job, nor should they. You should still put in the work and earn what you achieve yourself. Sometimes, however, you may only be given the chance to earn it with the boost of your network.

The social currency metaphor comes into play when thinking about asking for favors. A big ask is going to cost a lot of your social currency, possibly more than you have. You could destroy a lot of goodwill built over time if you are too greedy. If you spend a small amount of social currency on a small ask, you still have more saved for down the road and can even continue building up your stash.

What if I Know No One, Who Knows No One?

Early on, we talked about the ways networking intersects with privilege and socioeconomic status. It must be acknowledged again that, unfortunately, these two concepts naturally correspond. If you come from privilege, it is more likely that you will have easier access to a network of more privileged and powerful people. It's certainly a continuum, and I would contend that even if you're not in the upper range of people on that continuum, there are still ways to use the networking skills in this book.

However, the chapter on how to find people you want to know makes a lot of assumptions. For example, it assumes that you already have a helpful existing network and that you went to college. What if neither are the case?

New connections can truly come from anywhere. I know someone who grew up with little access to the resources that many of us have. No one in his family or his community has beyond a middle school level education. Through a connection of his former significant other, he got a job working for a local elected official while putting himself through college. Now he has a college degree and has several years under his belt working for a well-known and well-connected political figure in the community. He has a great relationship with his boss, and I know she loves him and would do anything for him (not a bad person to have in your corner!).

You never know where you'll find these connections. However, if you really don't think you have any access to anyone to help you get to where you want to go, you're going to have to take a little more initiative and be a little more creative.

If you are reading this book, you already have the initiative and the resolve to achieve your goals. With hard work, you will be successful. You just have to find ways to be inventive and build your network from scratch.

Let's say, for example, that you want to be an accountant. You don't know any accountants and no one you know knows any accountants. How can you meet an accountant? Well first of all, are you *sure* you have no second-degree connections to an accountant? Maybe you have no accountant relatives and neither do your friends. It's probable, though, that someone you know has used the services of a public accountant at some point. Think of your teachers at school, people from your religious community, and the parents of your friends. It's also likely someone you know works at a company that has an accounting department. Often, you may not think the connection is there, but you'll find one if you dig deep.

What if you want to be in finance or law or consulting or advertising and you know no one who knows no one? Lots of firms and companies have websites with employee profiles. Sometimes, their emails are even listed! Send a cold email explaining who you are, that you found their email on the company's website, and that you want to learn more about their job and field, but you don't know anyone who can help you. I bet they'll be blown away at the initiative and will be more than happy to be of help.

What if they don't respond? Try someone else! At some point, someone will respond and then you're well on your way. That one contact can open a whole world for you because that person knows people. If you ask if there's anyone else they know who you can talk to, they just might have someone for you.

Most people probably never even think about taking this level of initiative. Many people I have contacted from my school's alumni database have mentioned that they get emails from Penn students all the time wanting to chat. I bet you most professionals have never gotten a cold email from a complete stranger earnestly interested in learning from them. If one of the Penn alumni saw an email like that in between ten other ones from Penn students, I bet you that's the one they'd respond to first.

The system is definitely inequitable. It is unfair that some people have to work so much harder than others just to meet the right people. But by being creative and showing initiative, you prove that you have what it takes. No matter where you come from, you can succeed at networking despite barriers in your way. The hardest part is that first connection. Then, the doors will begin to open. Your first ally will lead to more and more as your community is built. Once you know that first person, you will never know no one who knows no one again.

Overzealous Networking

By now you've probably realized that networking takes putting yourself out there. That's really scary for anyone, but especially for introverts. Networking requires you to be outgoing. If you're uncomfortable talking to strangers, it's even harder to network. It would be a shame, however, to fall into a trap of thinking that networking is only for extraverts and you'll never be able to keep up with people to whom it comes naturally.

Yes, networking requires you to be a little forward, but it doesn't mean you have to make grand gestures. You don't have to be the kind of person that always wants to meet new people in order to meet new people.

I would consider myself more of an extravert than an introvert, but I am not someone who is always interested in meeting new people. I do not strike up conversations with people standing in line near me. I do not talk to people I'm sitting with on airplanes. You do not have to do things like that in order to be a successful networker. I would contend that an extravert can do all these things and may *still* not be a successful networker.

It's a similar idea to the art form of keeping in touch. The goal of your networking is to be effective, not just meet as many people as possible. Overzealous networking does not necessarily mean effective networking. In fact, it could have a negative effect.

This may sound contrary to what this book has discussed thus far, but you do not have to be extremely bold. Yes, you have to be bold enough to reach out to people and ask to learn from them, but I'm thinking of bold gestures. If there's someone you really want to meet, don't think that showing up to their office and saying you'll wait as long it takes to get five minutes with them will be an effective way to network. They won't be impressed with your tenacity and initiative. Instead, they may just call security on you. Boldest doesn't necessarily equal best.

In college, I once went on a trip to Los Angeles during spring break with a group of students to learn about the entertainment industry. We visited several major entertainment companies and met with Penn alumni working throughout the industry as producers, agents, and even in film finance. We were encouraged to ask as many questions as we could. The school even teased us that in the past, a few students were offered internships from the alumni they met, sometimes *while* on the trip itself.

There were over 30 of us, and everyone seemed to be there to get an internship. Everyone was trying to impress every speaker at every company. Someone would ask a question and the speaker would answer, and a half second after they'd finish, dozens of hands would shoot up in the air, fighting to be called on. The students couldn't have truly been listening to the answer. They just wanted to ask an insightful question to impress the speaker.

At the end of every presentation, my fellow students would practically rush the alumni and circle around them to ask more questions and have a more intimate chance to impress them. It felt like I was competing against everyone else for the attention of the alumni we were meeting. However, because so many people were trying to do the same thing, no one was sticking out, and it was unlikely these alumni were going to be particularly impressed by any one person. It was all a wash.

You might be thinking that this goes directly against the earlier section about asking questions at speaker events and going up to them afterwards to make another impression. After all, that's what all these kids were doing, right? If everyone was doing it, though, were they standing out from the crowd? What would I have gained from fighting my classmates for attention from the alumni? In that situation, they're most likely not going to remember which one of the many kids I was anyway.

This may be a little pessimistic. I'm sure that many, if not most, of the students on that trip genuinely were there to learn and asked questions to which they truly wanted answers. To me, the whole experience felt intense and stressful, like everyone's future depended on the questions they were asking. I realized that this was not true, and that I didn't need to put myself through that stress in order to be effective with my networking.

Being loud and bold does not always carry the day. The truly effective networkers are conscientious, kind, deliberate, and find ways to make impressions in appropriate ways. No matter where you are on the extraversion-to-introversion spectrum, you can find ways that work for you. You may have to go out of your comfort zone, but you can do it in a way that feels right and is effective for reaching your goals.

Network with Your Peers

Much of the networking strategies covered in this book involve reaching out to people who are in superior professional roles. Usually they're older and more experienced people who can teach you things and help you along the way. These connections can be very important, but you should not ignore your peers, who are equally, if not more important!

There's a tendency to feel the need to compete against peers, especially if you have similar goals. In many cases, only one person can get the job, right? You feel the need to beat out others. For peers, you have to shift from competition-mode to collaboration-mode. Especially when you're in the same industry, your peers will be the people you work with the longest. Why hurt your chances of a meaningful, fulfilling relationship over a long period of time because you were competing for the same job when you were young? The word "allies" is in the definition of networking for a reason. To reiterate, you should always strive to make allies and avoid making enemies when possible.

Young professionals in the entertainment industry learn the value of networking with peers early on. I've talked to many people in informational interviews who discussed how fruitful their first job at a talent agency was. Agencies often staff their mailroom (the place nearly everyone starts) in groups or "classes." These classes go through the mailroom process together, slowly get hired to work as agents' assistants throughout the company, and then they split up. Some go to work at studios, production companies, networks, and film financing. Some work in animation, writing, directing, producing, acting, or talent management, and some stay at the agency and get promoted to become agents themselves. Suddenly, a former mailroom clerk will know people in different roles in different companies all over Hollywood. It will be much easier to do business because they know the right people at the right places.

Don't forget that everyone you have met in your life is in your network. Make sure you're keeping in touch with people you know and are aware of what they're up to. You have a shared history so you most likely desire to share in each other's success. Your friends and classmates are a very sizable and very important part of your network, and they should be cultivated just like people who might seem like they could be more helpful in the immediate future.

The Networker's Lifestyle

One of my other favorite books I've read on networking is *Never Eat Alone* by Keith Ferrazzi. He is truly a master at networking and has been able to keep up with thousands of contacts throughout his life. One of my biggest takeaways from his book is that networking is a lifestyle and there are ways to incorporate it into your daily life. In my view, this requires thinking about other people. Thoughts like, "How is _____ doing?" and "I haven't heard from _____ in a while," are part of the networker's day-to-day life. The following are some other good mindsets to have when developing your own networking lifestyle.

Don't Delete Contacts!

I'm proud that since I got my first cell phone for my 12th birthday, I have never lost my contacts. The ones I added in 2008 are still there to this day. Meanwhile, many people I know have had all their contacts get erased in different sorts of accidents. I feel for them, because it's hard to recreate that whole list.

What I don't understand is people who intentionally delete contacts they feel they won't be needing anymore. Why would you do that? You never know when you might want to contact someone! Even if it does not seem like it, you truly never know when someone may pop up in your life again. It does not make you look exclusive or cool to have a limited number of contacts. The same goes for people who do most of their texting with phone numbers never saved in their phone. Why? It doesn't make sense to me. Keeping a well-organized and well curated contact list in your phone is crucial to networking.

When I was young, my friends used to make fun of me for how formally my contacts are labeled in my phone. I have a first and last name for everyone. Even my aunts and uncles are listed as "Aunt/Uncle FirstName LastName." No nicknames, no emojis. Just the first and last name. I'm not telling you that you need to do it this way. You can have as much fun with your contacts as you want, but make sure at the end of the day, you keep them in your phone!

I think this goes for friends on social media as well, particularly Facebook. I have witnessed a lot of Facebook purges, some of which I have survived and some of which I haven't. I get that some people are annoying on social media and especially if you don't know them very well, it can be very tempting to unfriend someone. You don't have to though! There's mute and block options for a reason. You can silence them on your feed and they'll never know, continuing to think they're your Facebook friend. This way, you can still reach out to them if you ever need to!

Of course, none of this is absolute. If you need to cut a truly toxic person out of your life, then of course you should do what you need to do. That should be an exception, though. People who you may not speak to very often and don't think you'll ever see again don't necessarily deserve to be kicked to the curb. You truly never know when you'll cross paths with someone. If you haven't spoken in a while, it may be a good opportunity to reach out!

By the way, make sure all your contacts are saved and backed up to a cloud-based storage system. If you ever get a new phone, your contacts should be able to follow you. Losing all of them would be a networking disaster!

Birthdays

I've heard people say that they find it extremely satisfying to unfriend someone on Facebook on their birthday. How cruel! This happens because birthdays pop up on the side of your Facebook news feed. For many people, they are reminded of connections they don't care about anymore. Instead of disconnecting, birthdays are actually the perfect time for reconnecting!

People love to be thought of on their birthday. Reaching out and wishing someone a happy birthday can really make their day special, especially if they haven't heard from you in a while. My favorite part of my birthday every year is hearing from friends and family, and the people I am most surprised to hear from are the ones that often mean the most. It takes just a few seconds to reach out to someone but it can really have a lasting impact.

Facebook is helpful here because you can see in the sidebar who among your friends has a birthday. I also get emails from Facebook every morning telling me whose birthday it is that day. Posting on their timeline is great, but I think sending a direct message makes an even bigger impact.

In addition to Facebook, I keep a birthday calendar in my phone. You can add someone's birthday in their contact, and it automatically syncs with the calendar app so you see can whose birthday it is every day. I never miss birthdays, and I would encourage keeping them in your calendar in addition to Facebook.

Pinging

Pinging is another thing I learned from Keith Ferrazzi's book, *Never Eat Alone*. It refers to sending a little message via text or email to someone just to say hi. It's similar to the concept of keeping in touch with new contacts discussed in an earlier chapter. Instead of sending an article, you just send a short message, such as, "hey thinking of you, hope all is well."

Pinging works really well for messages of congratulations. "Hey, saw you landed that big promotion, congrats!" It's also good to ping someone if something you experience makes you think of them. If you hear a song, go to a place, or see something that reminds you of a memory you share with that person, it's a great reason to reach out to them.

This practice is better for peers and relatives than those contacts with whom you've had an informational interview. It's a way to maintain your relationships. There are some people I'd imagine you don't need to ping, as you talk to them often. Use pinging to reach that next group of people who aren't your close inner circle but are still good friends with whom you'd like to stay in contact.

Connecting Others

I should hope this would go without saying, but one who lives the networker's lifestyle is always looking for ways to use networking to be helpful in others' lives. Use your network to bring people together! If you have two friends who don't know each other but have similar interests, offer to introduce them! Don't wait to be asked.

With their permission, you should also find ways to connect your friends to others you know for informational interviews when possible. Many of my relatives are lawyers, most of whom practice different areas of law. Whenever I encounter a friend who is interested in going to law school, I always offer to connect them with someone in my family who may be helpful.

Beyond professional interests, there are other reasons to connect people. One of the proudest connections I made was when I introduced my cousin and a camp friend who were going to the same university.

After they talked, they decided to become freshman roommates!

Remember, you reap what you sow. If you are someone who is proactive and excited to make connections for people and help them use networking to achieve their goals, then they will be more likely to return the favor. You'll become known as the networker in your network, and people will start to turn to you to see if you know anyone who can help them. This is a good reputation to have, because people who are known for being well-connected are also known for being both "in the know" and for being someone people *want* to know!

Keeping Track of Everyone and Everything

When you have so many people you're connecting with, it's important to stay organized. Otherwise, you won't be able to keep up with who is who and where you are in your correspondence.

It is helpful to have a folder in your email inbox labeled "Networking" to keep track of all your emails with potential new contacts. Sometimes when I want to reach out to someone I haven't communicated with for a while, I'll go back to our last email and respond on that thread to refresh their memory of who I am.

I also utilize spreadsheets to help keep track of my networking. When I began researching people to reach out to from my college alumni database, I listed them and their information on a spreadsheet. I made notes about what date I emailed them and when they responded. This helped me keep track of who needed a follow-up. I added new sheets to the document after each summer internship. I made notes about what reasons I might have for reaching out to contacts from the summer and what topics I could bring up in the coming year. When I did connect, I noted the date and any further information.

When I moved to Los Angeles permanently, the spreadsheet became more intense. I did not have a full-time job, so I spent all my time applying, following up, interviewing, and networking. I added a new spreadsheet to keep up with all of this, making detailed notes about every meeting I had. The people needing further follow-up were highlighted yellow until those tasks were completed.

This may sound like too much work, and if you don't think you need to do this in order to keep track of your networking, then that's great. Find a system that works for you and stick to it. Don't let your networking fall through the cracks, though. You have to be on your game because people will, without meaning to, let *you* fall through the cracks, and you want to prevent that.

Joining Groups and Attending Networking Events

One great way to meet new contacts is through joining various groups. Getting involved in a group or an activity is something we did all the time as kids, teens, and even in college. We played sports, sang in choirs, participated in religious youth groups, and more. They were great because we made friends with common interests, and the same is true as an adult as well. Being involved in an organization or an activity provides fantastic networking opportunities.

Rotary clubs, bar associations, and other professional societies are great ways to network with others in the local community. They provide opportunities for professional development in addition to meeting new people. My father used to attend the local dermatological society meetings once a month and learned from speakers while networking with other local dermatologists. When my mother first moved to Phoenix after law school, she joined the Jewish Business and Professional Women. This allowed her to create a community in her new city. Many of the connections she made are still friends to this day. These clubs are fantastic ways to make meaningful relationships.

Sometimes, a particular organization may sponsor a one-off networking event. These are often happy hours where people arrive, put on name tags, and participate in unstructured mingling. They're often attended by people who are looking for work. Some colleges host similar networking events for alumni. I've been to a few of them. This is what I call forced networking, and it really is not ideal. It can be awkward and the people who attend don't often have the best attitude about networking. They might just need a job. Learning and building a community of allies may not be at the top of the priority list. Everyone is out for themselves. This is not a recipe for successful networking.

These events shouldn't necessarily be avoided, but don't have high expectations. It will always be a valuable experience because you will meet new people and that automatically expands your network, but you may not enjoy it. Networking should be enjoyable if you're doing it right!

The best networking happens in settings that were not specifically designed for people to network. Gyms and intramural sports leagues, religious organizations, community arts, and other nonprofit organizations are fantastic ways to network with like-minded people. It is easy to form strong bonds with people in these settings because the connecting happens during a shared non-professional interest.

When I was a senior in high school, I served as a trustee on the board of the Jewish Community Foundation of Greater Phoenix. I was a liaison to the foundation's youth philanthropy board. This organization was (and still is) dedicated to helping fund programs and services at other local Jewish organizations. The board consisted of a variety of local Jewish professionals who were passionate about supporting the Jewish community. There were doctors, lawyers, financial advisors, entrepreneurs, homemakers, real estate developers, and clergy on the board. This was a great way for the board members to network with other local professionals while bonding over a shared interest, the Jewish community. The philanthropy came first, the networking came second.

Joining any group is good for networking, but attending events designed specifically for networking may be less rewarding. Often, lasting connections are made in groups where networking is a secondary purpose. Interest groups where the members share a common passion are great places to create community.

An Attitude of Gratitude

I saved the most important lesson for last. Every day, in every way, with everyone we come across, it's imperative to show an attitude of gratitude. Building a network when you're young only happens because of the generosity of others, and we should be thankful for that.

This is a book about networking for young people early in their career. When established professionals think about networking, they are looking to connect with people with whom they can do business. Young people like us are further down the professional totem pole and we don't have the experience, skills, or ability to offer very much to these professionals. When we're connecting with people to learn and get a little boost to get a job or achieve another professional goal, we receive the vast majority of the benefit. We need them far more than they need us. Usually, they don't need us at all.

Given that, the only reason why a person would waste even a second of their time talking to us is because they are a kind and generous person who is willing to help out the next generation. They remember what it was like when they were our age and they want to help out from the goodness of their heart.

We have to recognize this. We have to internalize and understand how unequal these networking relationships are when we're young. We have to be grateful for the opportunities we have to connect with truly amazing people. That's why there's a whole chapter in this book about writing thank-you notes, but it goes beyond that. It's about living your life being grateful that the world is filled with kind-hearted people who are willing to be generous with their time and knowledge. New professional contacts are lending a helping hand to someone they know can't offer much in return. It's about having an attitude of gratitude.

Paying it Forward

It's likely that we will not be able to return all the favors we will get. We can't truly repay all the gracious people who helped us along the way. Instead, we will pay it forward to the next generation of young people who will find themselves trying to make it in the world. Before we know it, you and I will be successful professionals, and young people will come to us seeking knowledge and maybe a little help along the way. They will want us to be in their network. Because we will remember this time in our lives, when we relied on the generosity of others, we will do the same.

I bet the reason why people are willing to connect with us now is because they are paying it forward too. When they were our age, they too relied on the generosity of others to learn and build a network, and now it's their turn to help the next generation.

I must hearken back to those values I learned at my camp as a teen. One of them was **generational leadership**. Know before whom you stand. In learning from those who came before us, we must work to ensure our hard work lives on. We are a product of our network, and we will help produce a new generation of supportive collaborators who are interested in building community and working together so they can share in the success of their allies.

We will show our gratitude by continuing to create and build community. We will pay it forward.

Conclusion

Networking is the work of creating and building a community of supportive collaborators and allies with common interests who desire to share in each other's success.

No one can truly succeed alone in this world. We succeed together as a community. The best networkers are those who care about the others in their network, genuinely want to see them succeed, and are willing to do what they can to help. Networking has the word "work" in it for a reason. It most certainly takes work and it is work that never ends. It is emotionally nourishing work, because it's the people's work.

Having relationships takes work. Being in a community takes work. Loving and caring takes work, but it is what makes life sweet. Being with other human beings we care about is what gives us meaning and what keeps us going when adversity strikes.

This is networking. It should never, ever be a self-serving endeavor. Those who network selfishly will not be successful in the long run because they will fail to build a meaningful community. Those who network with intention and are focused on the "we" rather than the "I" will reap the benefits of supporting others and finding joy in their success.

I hope this book helps you see networking in a new way and gives you some tools to utilize your innate networking abilities to your full advantage. No matter where you come from, you will need to network in order to achieve your goals, and you have the power to make it happen. I am also a young person early in my career just like you. I am still figuring my life out and leaning on others for guidance. This book reflects what I have learned about networking from the generous people who have taught and helped me along the way, and I am grateful to everyone in my network who has supported me in all my endeavors past, present, and future.

To revisit one of my favorite values, **every person is the most important person in the world to someone.** Networking is about seeing the inherent value in every human being and treating them with the kindness, respect, and generosity they deserve. This attitude is what it takes to create the kind of community we want our networks to be. Let's commit to networking with generosity and integrity. Let's network to create a supportive and collaborative community made of people we care about. That's what matters in the end.

And in the end, it's who you know.

About the Author

Scott Rubenstein is a young adult living and working in New York, New York. Originally from Scottsdale, Arizona, he graduated from the University of Pennsylvania in 2019 with a degree in Communication, a concentration in Political Communication, and a minor in Political Science. This is his first book.

www.ingramcontent.com/pod-product-compliance
Lightning Source LLC
Chambersburg PA
CBHW032211220526
45472CB00018B/1127